LARGER THAN AN ORANGE

LARGER THAN AN ORANGE

Lucy Burns

Chatto & Windus
LONDON

1 3 5 7 9 10 8 6 4 2

Chatto & Windus, an imprint of Vintage, is part of the
Penguin Random House group of companies whose addresses
can be found at global.penguinrandomhouse.com

Penguin
Random House
UK

Copyright © Lucy Burns 2021

Lucy Burns has asserted her right to be identified as the author
of this Work in accordance with the Copyright, Designs and
Patents Act 1988

First published by Chatto & Windus in 2021

penguin.co.uk/vintage

A CIP catalogue record for this book is available from the British Library

ISBN 9781784744410

Medical definitions on pages 190–1 and 193–4 are taken from Jonathan Law and
Elizabeth Martin, eds., *The Oxford Concise Medical Dictionary* (10th edition)
(Oxford University Press, 2020)

Typeset in 11/14 pt Minion Pro
by Integra Software Services Pvt. Ltd, Pondicherry

Printed and bound in Great Britain by Clays Ltd, Elcograf S.p.A.

The authorised representative in the EEA is Penguin Random House Ireland,
Morrison Chambers, 32 Nassau Street, Dublin D02 YH68

Penguin Random House is committed to a sustainable future for
our business, our readers and our planet. This book is made from
Forest Stewardship Council® certified paper.

MIX
Paper from
responsible sources
FSC
www.fsc.org   FSC® C018179

To Emily

It's his turn to do it. He flips open the lid and peers inside the wheelie bin. The air is hot and trashy. Several months of discharge, compressed into discrete fatty layers. He is partially responsible for this mess, he thinks.

First: bleach.

Second: boiling water. The plastic relaxes slightly in his hands. Chili con carne, the toilets at the swimming pool, sauerkraut.

Third: the hose. It takes a while. Gobs of oil shuffle and divide. He knows he shouldn't, but everyone does. He dips the bin, like he's dancing with it, and pours it into the street. Chunks cling to the drain cover. The fatberg at the end of the street is fortified. He wipes his hands.

Later that night (though he'll never see it): an orange smudge inside the back pocket of his jeans, where the colour has lifted.

'I want to arrange a termination.'

'You mean an *abortion*.'

One.

After providing details of how I'd gotten pregnant ('I'm afraid I'm going to need a bit more information than that'), my current relationship status, last period, dates of any sexual activity in the last two months, average menstrual-cycle length, when I had taken the morning-after pill, where it had been administered, weight, height, second-to-last period, last visit to a sexual health clinic, NHS number ('you must bring this with you'), contraceptive history, reasons for choosing a medical rather than surgical abortion, name and address of General Practitioner ('you'll need to find out'), date of pregnancy test ('can you repeat that?'), date of pregnancy test, number of pregnancy tests consulted, and the results of the pregnancy tests, I am told there is an appointment at a nearby clinic later today, where the first set of drugs can be administered that afternoon.

'You must drink a litre of water one hour before the appointment.'

All day, desperate to touch each other.

We haven't seen each other in five or six years, but there's the taper down the back of his neck, the belt strap drawing steadily through the loop.

I don't want to have to think about it.

He wasn't supposed to, but he did.

I stay up with my phone, trying to find somewhere I can get the morning-after pill on a Sunday.

Closed.

Midday.

Closed.

I find a pharmacy that opens early. He walks me to the bus stop and offers to pay. I know he hasn't got any cash.

In the pharmacy, there is a queue of people in yesterday's clothes. We sit quietly, with our hands in our laps (no battery), waiting to be called in to explain ourselves.

I'm pregnant, I message him. I wait a second, then add: *not a joke.*

Two.

There is no discussion. He apologises again. I tell him I've already arranged the abortion and that I'll call when it's done.

When [----] answers the phone, I say something like: 'I'm pregnant but I've arranged an abortion.'

Three.

I can tell she is late for work. She is furious. Breathlessly: What happened? Whose is it? Why did you do that? Why did you let him do that? Why have you done this to yourself? How could you have been so fucking stupid?

I want to tell her to stand still. I hang up.

Three people know about the abortion.

I message [----] to ask if he's free. A few minutes later, when I can see he's read it but hasn't replied, I add: *not like, free for a pint free, but free to come to an abortion clinic.*

Four.

I'm trying to be light-hearted, but I suddenly feel flippant and ashamed. I want to make another joke to cancel it out.

Four agrees to come to the clinic with me. I send him the address and we agree to meet in a café nearby.

I sit facing the direction I know he'll appear from.

He rounds the corner: head down, marching, like he's already late. An unopened, two-litre bottle of water is wedged under his armpit. I'm not sure if it's because it's hot, or because he knows about the ultrasound. I don't ask.

The first thing he says, catching his breath, is: 'You can tell me as much or as little as you want.'

He doesn't order anything.

I tell him that it's going to be OK.

He lightly compresses the bottle with his fingertips while I talk.

I tell him that it's definitely going to be OK! That it's obviously the right decision, the only decision   actually it's not even a decision, really! it's just what's going to happen I've worked it out and I'm only three and a half weeks pregnant   I only had sex three and a half weeks ago! so it's basically just a ball of cells at this point

We look down at my phone and up at the building. We look down at my phone and up at the building. We've walked past the clinic hundreds of times before and never noticed it. I'm not sure what I expected. People at the bus stop opposite watch us figure it out.

There are security bars on the windows and a small sign above the doorway, which is half closed. We crowd into the little porch and I pull the handle. The door is locked. The receptionist glances up from the desk. I scan the faces in the waiting room. I press the buzzer.

'I have an appointment at twelve thirty.'

The door is unlocked.

Everyone is drinking water. The blinds are drawn. The fan has been unplugged. The television on the wall whines faintly. I am handed a clipboard and some literature.

All the seats are taken, so we huddle together in the middle of the room. I rest the clipboard against FOUR's back.

EARLY MEDICAL ABORTION

The receptionist exchanges the information on the clipboard for a pink raffle ticket. I look at it blankly.

'So there are no names,' she says.

I go back to the middle of the room and FOUR brings me a cup of water. We shuffle around each other, like showgirls, to face the television screen.

FOUR tries to make a joke about the programme and I move my mouth into a smile, but I'm not sure if I should laugh or shush.

I alternate between my left hand (plastic cup) and my right (water bottle). FOUR holds the bottle lid and my raffle ticket in his open, upturned palm. I wonder if anyone has noticed his wedding ring.

I occasionally raise one of the flyers to my face in case the receptionist is watching and this is part of a test.

The water cooler chugs.

FOUR keeps his eyes on the television screen.

Four brings me a cup of water. Someone new arrives. The waiting room examines their shoes. I refill the cup.

How many times a week do they have to change the tank on the water cooler? How do they get the bottle upside down without spilling it everywhere? What happens when it runs out? Does the receptionist change it herself? She probably doesn't have time. Maybe the water cooler company sends someone.

Four brings me a cup of water. We take it in turns to stare at a sign:

NO CHILDREN ALLOWED IN THE WAITING ROOM

My number is called.

I take the damp raffle ticket from Four's hand. I don't want him to be here anymore. I give him my bag and jacket and tell him to go wait in the café.

I've drunk so much I can barely walk. I waddle into the dark room. It is larger than I expected. The door is locked behind me.

'Lie on the bed.'

The only light in the room is a medical lamp next to the ultrasound machine. The technician sits down at the computer and watches me get on the bed. I cast a huge shadow across the room.

'Lower your trousers.'

I lean back, exhaling in sharp bursts. She makes it clear she is waiting. I unbutton my jeans and start to lower them.

'No –'

She tuts and grabs at the waistband.

You're going to piss yourself.

I pull my jeans back up. I try to work out what she wants me to do. I know I'm not supposed to ask. I fold the pockets of my jeans out and look across at her for approval.

'No. Like this –'

She reaches for my jeans. I flinch, then apologise. She folds the waistband over and tucks a piece of tissue into the top of my underwear. I keep very still. She squeezes something onto my belly and presses the sensor down.

You're going to piss yourself.

The screen is turned away. She says nothing. The wand ploughs back and forth. This is not about me.

'When did you take the test?'

'This morning.'

She pushes down harder. I exhale steadily.

'Right. And you're sure the test was positive?'

'Yes.'

'I can't see anything. You'll need to come back in ten days.'

I say nothing. She turns away and adjusts the height of her chair. It occurs to me that I already know what I'll do if I'm pregnant for ten more days. I'm disappointed by how obvious it is. She fusses the machine.

'Or we can do a transvaginal ultrasound.'

The probe makes a brief appearance, wearing an enormous condom. It is inserted into the vagina. I try not to think about why I'm crying. The ultrasound technician forces the probe against the cervix, then pulls it around the walls of the vagina. I don't want her to know that it hurts.

The probe is removed. I await my next instruction. She says nothing. I close and flatten the legs. She types at the computer. Something is being printed. I button my jeans and sit up. I take my shoes out from under the chair.

'Did that show what it needed to?'

'Yes.'

'What happens now?'

'Go back to the waiting room and wait for your number to be called.'

The television has been unmuted. I try to work out who else has experienced the ultrasound room. I decide it's better not to look at anyone.

I pick up a leaflet called *Considering abortion?* and move my eyes around the pages. I consider how I might perform indecision, if I have to.

Someone pulls at the door and the waiting room looks up. The delivery driver presses the buzzer. The door is unlocked. They pass a clipboard to the receptionist.

I examine the deteriorating condition of the pink raffle ticket.

Someone appears from a different door and calls my number.

No sex for four weeks. No exercise for four weeks. No swim-ming for four weeks. No – I wouldn't ride a bike. No lifting heavy objects. No grapefruit. No grapefruit juice. No aspirin. No alcohol. Do not take this pregnancy test until four weeks after your last appointment. No mefenamic acid. No St John's wort. No alcohol. Would you like the abortion to appear on your medical records? Why not? Do not use public transport after the procedure. You must not use tampons. You must call a taxi. Do not insert *anything* into the vagina. No bathing. No recreational drugs. No smoking. Avoid tea and coffee. Avoid tight or fitted clothing. You must not walk home from the clinic after the second appointment. You should have some-one waiting for you at home. No sexual activity. When you get home, you will feel the need to push. When this happens: Go to the toilet, sit down on the toilet, and bear down. When you're finished, don't look in the toilet bowl. Just flush.

I am given a pink, stripy pick 'n' mix bag. The nurse packs it in front of me: copies of the leaflets we know you didn't read in the waiting room, the private phone number of the clinic, an appointment card for tomorrow, carbon copies of the forms you don't remember signing, and a pregnancy test. She takes a long string of condoms from a tray on the desk, stuffs them into the bag, and hands it to me.

I float to the café and sit down and exhale jaggedly and shake my head and try to stop crying. Four asks what happened.

I have to go back tomorrow   I have to go back tomorrow and then the day after that 'why are you here?' 'why do you want an abortion?' she said I would have to come back in ten days unless I had to say 'don't look!' it was like I had to beg 'just flush the toilet!' what the fuck

The waitress circles past. I stop talking. Four has never seen me cry before. I wish he wasn't there again. I want to be humiliated in private. He asks if I've eaten. I wipe my face on my shoulder and get up to order something. At the counter, I notice that a wet smear of ultrasound gel has soaked through my shirt.

The sandwich arrives. I sit up to inspect it. There's nothing to talk about anymore. I should never have told anyone. I consider the sandwich for a minute, then tell Four he should have it.

I tell him not to come tomorrow.

When I get home, I immediately throw out the condoms. I tear up the signed forms and separate them into different bin bags.

I spend the evening cross-checking what I can remember from the consultation room with advice on the internet from other abortion clinics and charities.

Do not use bubble bath or bath salts for at least three weeks after the treatment. No bathing for forty-eight hours. We advise that you avoid any heavy lifting or exercise for two to three weeks. Take two paracetamol and two ibuprofen before your second appointment. Do not take any paracetamol or ibuprofen before your second appointment. Your breasts may feel firm or tender or leak after your procedure. We recommend you have someone stay with you overnight. No sex for two weeks. Refrain from sexual intercourse for three weeks after the treatment. Once you feel sufficiently recovered, you can return to having sex. It is important to use contraception immediately after the procedure if you don't want to get pregnant again. It is inadvisable for you to change your mind once the first tablet has been taken. After an abortion most women feel relieved, but some may feel sad or guilty. Go to the hospital if you pass something larger than an orange.

It's late when I remember to call Two.

There is some confusion. We are careful not to call it into being.

'You have to go back?'

'Yes.'

'Tomorrow?'

'Yes, tomorrow and then again the day after that.'

I tell him I'll call after my second appointment.

'We need to make a decision today,' I say.

The colleague drags my notepad across the table. He points at what I've written. I squeeze my hands together and try to explain the schedule again. The line manager takes an orange from the bag under his desk. He peels it in a single twist.

'We really need to finalise this today,' I say.

The conversation continues. The notepad slides around the table. I check my watch.

'I have a hospital appointment tomorrow,' I interrupt unexpectedly, 'so I'll need to finish this tonight.'

'Nothing serious, I hope?'

'No. But we need to make a final decision today.'

When the meeting sounds like it could be finishing, I snatch the notepad and walk out.

'Great I'll finish it tonight thanks bye!'

The line manager calls down the corridor, but I keep walking.

I arrive at the clinic just in time for my appointment. They are running behind schedule. In the waiting room, I draft an email to the line manager to apologise for my behaviour.

First: When you're ready, take this tablet. This will stop the pregnancy from developing any further.

Second: Go to the toilet and insert this painkiller in your anus. Wear this glove, then dispose of it.

Third: Take this antibiotic home with you. It will make you feel sick. Swallow it an hour before bed, so you sleep through the nausea. You must, at all costs, resist the urge to be sick. If you vomit within an hour of swallowing the tablet, you will have to come back to the clinic and start the process again. If you vomit within two to three hours, the chances of having a successful abortion decrease significantly. When you come back for the next appointment, tomorrow, you must tell the nurse whether or not you have been sick.

I sit in the dark and finish the work project. I know I should take the tablet and go to bed, but I stay up for a while with my emails.

> Reply
>
> *I won't be at my desk tomorrow, but I'll get to this as soon as I can.*
>
> Send
>
> Delete
>
> Delete

I switch to my personal inbox.

> Search: From: Two
>
> Delete
>
> To: Two
>
> Delete
>
> "Two"
>
> Delete

I unlock my phone and delete his phone number. I delete the messages. I take the antibiotic and get into bed.

I still haven't slept *hot* *this is it* *sit up* 'Jesus Christ what have I done?' *need to move* *can't be sick on the bed* *'sleep through the nausea'* *how long did she say you had to keep it down?* *where's your phone?* *what was it called?* *what have you taken?* 'if I'm sick –' *keep it down* *keep it down* 'I'm going to be OK I'm not going to be sick' *oh god what's happening* 'if I'm sick –' *you can't do this again* *you can't take time off* *you can't do it* *you're gonna have to do this all over again* *open the window* 'come on! get a fucking grip! it's passing I'm not gonna be sick I'm not gonna be sick' *this is going to pass* *get a flannel* *look at yourself* *this is going to pass* Jesus *you can't keep it down* *you can't do it* 'I can't do it' *why is no one here with you?* *why are you on your own?* *you have no one* 'I have no one' *you have no one* 'I don't need anyone' *you can't do this on your own* 'fucking bitch' *water* *sit down* *tie your hair back* *take your top off* *wet the flannel* 'bitch!' *calm down* 'calm calm' *look at what you've done to yourself* 'don't retch' *don't fucking retch* 'I want my mum' *you have no one* 'sit up' *breathe* *sip* 'I want my dad' *calm* 'no' *cold* *get a towel* 'If I'm sick Jesus if I'm sick' *sit still* *what did she say?* *what the fuck did you take?* *why have you done this?* 'bitch' *is this supposed to happen?* *you need to call someone* *where's your phone?* 'still' *sit still* *close the window* 'calm down calm down' *you're going to be OK* 'I'm going to be OK' *sip* *where's the flannel?* *take your trousers off* *hot* *this is it* *this is it* 'stop it' *here it comes* 'breathe' *this is it* 'calm' *fuck* 'I feel so bad' *you have no*

26

one 'stop it stop crying' *you're gonna throw up if you're sick* 'what the fuck is going on?' *you can't do this* 'I can't do this' *keep it down* 'fucking come on!' *it'll pass* 'it's passing it's passing' *open the window* 'it's passing it's passing' *look at what you've done to yourself* 'it's passing it's passing it's passing' *lie down*

I wake up under the towel on the sofa. The sun is coming up. I put my pyjamas back on and go to bed for a few hours.

When I push down on the egg, a thin, milky liquid bursts across the plate. I lift up the roof of the collapsed egg with the tip of the knife and scrape out the remains. The yolk is perfectly intact. It slides off the plate into the open bin.

The television hasn't been turned on yet. I'm the only person in the waiting room.

I check in for my appointment and accidentally sit down by the door, which means I'm the first person someone sees when they arrive. I gaze at the bench on the other side of the room.

Someone pulls the handle and I resist the urge to look up. They press the buzzer. The door unlocks. I read the same paragraph in my book again.

My number is called.

The nurse works through the checklist. I wait to be asked if I've been sick.

She tells me that because it's been less than twenty-four hours since the first drug was administered, I should come back later. Tomorrow even.

'Why wasn't I told this yesterday?'

'You were.'

I don't remember. I cry again while she writes down a series of percentages indicating the success rates at less than twenty-four hours, between twenty-four and forty-eight hours, and after forty-eight hours. She turns the piece of paper round to face me and waits for my decision. I pretend I am thinking about it.

'No. Let's do it now.'

'Take off your trousers and underwear and lie down on the bed, with your knees apart and your heels tucked underneath your bottom.'

The bars on the windows. The gap in the blinds near the ceiling. The white examination light, bent over the bed. The mirrored concentric circles inside the lamp.

Five, if you count the receptionist.

Six, if you count the ultrasound technician.

Seven, if you count the first nurse.

Eight.

Nine.

From this angle: the gap at the bottom of the blinds and the alley outside.

Now, this angle: the reflection of the strip lights on the wipe-clean floor.

She draws the curtain. I take a sanitary pad out of my bag and quietly stick it to my underwear.

My admission that I will be walking home is causing significant problems.

'You were told that you're not allowed to leave the clinic unless you've called a taxi.'

'I'm not allowed to leave?'

My face creeps helplessly into a smile. I explain that it's less than a ten-minute walk. I explain that it would take longer to call a taxi, wait for a taxi, and stop at a cashpoint on the way home than it would walk. I explain that I understand perfectly well all the reasons why the clinic has to tell me not to walk or take public transport, but in this instance, in this particular set of circumstances, it really is quicker for me to walk. I explain that if I go home right now, rather than talking about how I'm going to go home, I will be home in less than ten minutes.

I walk home like I'm carrying a large and expensive cake. Something hurts from the speculum, but I try not to think about where. Instead, I practise what I'll say to the stranger that helps me if I trip over, or faint, or get hit by a bus.

Next to the bed: two pints of water, box of tissues, washing up bowl, small towel, large towel, hot water bottle, phone charger.

Three or four hours pass. I watch *The Terminator*.

Night. The hydraulic frame eases over the front of the dumpster. The truck driver carefully aligns the forks.

Los Angeles 1984
1:52 a.m.

The engine strains. The headlight fizzes out. The driver reaches for the keys.

'What the hell? God damn son of a –'

A low hum. The wind picks up in the alley. Blue electricity discharges surround the truck. Snapping. Rustling. Dust. The driver winces and leans his head out the window.

'What the hell?'

The dumpster is suspended over the front of the truck. A flash, then surging. The driver unbuckles and jumps out of the cab.

The steam clears: the Cyberdyne Systems Model 101 Series 800 Terminator, healthy, 230lb 4oz.

Floodlights bounce off its hairless, perfectly formed body. It rises up and opens its eyes for the first time. The thin, greasy coating on its face comes into focus. It manoeuvres away from the truck and processes the city.

Something has started. I sit on the toilet and drip into the bowl. The blood doesn't look like menstrual blood. Maybe this is it, I think. I remember a phrase from my internet research: *like a heavy period*. Maybe it is like a heavy period. Maybe it will be like a heavy period.

Nothing hurts, but I make a hot water bottle anyway and lie down again.

Kyle Reese stuffs the pipe bomb into the holdall. His movements are hesitant; he is nervous about the scene. Sarah Connor walks over to him and holds the back of his neck in place just like they practised. She gently kisses him on the mouth. They slide down the side of the refrigerator. He puts his hands on her breasts and squeezes. Her body moves on top of his. They lock their hands together and pretend to come at the same time. The audience now understands Sarah Connor to be pregnant.

The T-800 powers towards the motel. His shotgun rests neatly on his shoulder.

I pretend to ignore it for a few minutes, but it's getting closer. I get up and sit on the edge of the bed. I am sweating and shivering. I open the window. Everything is happening very quickly. The pain spreads from my lower back, to my tailbone, to my pelvis.

I call [----]. We haven't spoken in a few months, but I need to talk to someone who knows me. Ringing. He picks up.

'I know you probably don't want to speak to me but I didn't know who else to call and –'

'What's happened?'

'I'm pregnant and I've had an abortion – I'm having an abortion.'

Ten.

I pace between the living room, the kitchen, the bathroom, the kitchen, the living room, the bathroom. TEN is on speaker-phone.

'I'm gonna be sick. I'm gonna be sick.'

I'm frightened by how frightened I sound. He tells me to calm down.

'I'm sorry for calling. I just don't know what's happening.'

TEN tells me to sit down. He's only pretending to be calm, but I listen to him anyway.

He is telling me to breathe slowly and I am listening to him and listening to him and then the pain gets worse and I am angry and desperate.

'*Jesus Christ* what have I done? What the fuck have I done to myself? I shouldn't have done this.'

He says nothing.

We're in the bathroom now. I hold onto the sink and rock from side to side. The wall braces.

'When will I feel better?'

Soon, he tells me. I'm snivelling now.

'Really?'

Another hour passes. I hang my head in the sink. Sweat drips forward. The sink amplifies my panting.

'I'm gonna be sick   I'm gonna be sick.'

I feel wet. The pain drops off. I get a colder cold flannel and am filling up the hot water bottle when it starts again. My legs shake.

'It's happening again!' I shout at my phone.

'Can you check if this is supposed to happen? Can you look this up?'

He says he will.

'Fuck, I'm gonna be sick.'

I take the washing up bowl into the living room.

'Are you still there?'

He is.

'I don't know what to do. *Please*.'

I'm heaving now. I clench my fists. I swallow and shake my head.

'When can I be sick? I can't remember what she said.'

He tells me that I'm not going to be sick, that the nausea will pass soon.

'I don't know what's happening! I can't believe I don't know.'

I grunt and lean forward. Too late. I vomit in the washing up bowl on the floor.

'I was just sick!' I shout.

TEN is reading out something from the internet. We sit together until the pain passes.

On the next break ('hang on a second') I tip the vomit into the toilet and am bleaching the washing up bowl when it starts again. I can hear him talking in the living room. I leave the bowl in the sink and stagger to the living room ('back').

Another hour passes. I want to be on my own again. He asks if I'm still there.

'Yeah. It's over, isn't it?'

He says he thinks so.

'That was it, wasn't it? I'm not going to feel worse again.'

No, he says, it's finished now.

I feel stupid for keeping him on the phone for so long.

'You're terminated, fucker!'

FOUR messages to ask if I want him to come over and cook dinner.

Yeah

I sit like a frog on the sofa and listen to FOUR sliding trays in and out of the oven. He has opened the window and the room feels breezy. I wonder if it was the bleach or the diarrhoea. The television is on mute. Sirens hover past. A tram meeps. Shutters roll closed.

FOUR refills my hot water bottle but forgets to burp it. I hold it between my knees and discreetly let the steam out. I suddenly imagine pouring it over myself. I ignore the thought. FOUR surrounds me with kitchen roll and vinegar and cutlery and salt. He hands me a plate of fish fingers, chips, and peas.

I turn the sound on and neither of us mention the raffle ticket or the water cooler or the *NO CHILDREN ALLOWED* sign and I'm saying: That was the worst experience of my life!

and then I'm saying: That was the worst thing I've ever done

and then I'm saying: It was just a ball of cells but   I'm obviously not anti-abortion but

I'm pro-abortion   I am   and I believe that anyone should be able to get an abortion if they want one   and abortion should be free and safe and legal   but I have just killed something that was living inside me

Hours and hours, waiting for something to happen. A slow accumulation of barely perceptible gestures. His weight shifting into the left side of his body. His eyes up to where my skirt begins. His hand underneath my knee, pulling me towards him.

The bedroom door crashes open. The T-800 pumps the shotgun.

I call in sick. When the line manager returns the call, I let it ring out.

This morning's headlines: British pharmacy chain refuse to cut cost of morning-after pill.

'We don't want to be seen to be incentivising inappropriate use.'

In the shower: carefully wash the face, the armpits, the feet. Right nipple is distended and points stage left. Invert it with an index finger. Remove the finger and watch it slowly inflate. Lather up the hands, wash them, then take the shower head off the wall and spray it between the legs.

I drop the last eggs into the bin. I think about making break-fast. Instead, I lie on my bed and cry.

What are you crying for? It's done.

I turn on the radio.

'Good afternoon. It's exactly fifty years since abortion was made *conditionally legal* in the United Kingdom, in a move that superseded the 1861 Offences Against the Person Act, which rendered a woman's attempt to "procure her own miscarriage" a crime. The 1967 Abortion Act was, and remains, one of the most controversial pieces of legislation in British history. Not just for its effective decriminalisation of the procedure, but in its omission of provisions for Northern Ireland, where women are forced to make the costly and potentially dangerous journey to mainland Britain to have an abortion. Today, nearly two hundred thousand abortions are carried out each year in England and Wales under "ground C", an exemption clause that permits abortion in instances where two doctors agree, in *good faith*, that there is a risk to the physical or mental health of the pregnant woman. While the legislation is hailed by pro-abortionists as a triumph for women's rights to bodily autonomy, anti-abortionists argue that the Abortion Act is being abused and innocent lives are being destroyed for matters of convenience. Both sides would have you believe that this is a straightforward issue: a matter of life and death, autonomy or coercion, reproductive justice or murder. But, recently, the fundamentals of the debate are being called into question again: At what point do we become human beings? Is the unborn foetus a person? And are these questions for science, philosophy, or the pregnant woman herself? On the fiftieth anniversary of the Abortion Act, we're returning to some of the issues at the heart of this complex and emotive topic. Let's meet our panel.'

I imagine all the people in taxis at traffic lights and in kitchens and waiting rooms and open-plan offices and on toilets and sofas in the middle of the day, all desperately straining not to listen.

I check my diary and realise that [----] and [----] are supposed to come over for dinner tonight. I draft a series of messages:

> *I think we'll have to cancel tonight*
>
> *I had a procedure yesterday*
>
> *I had an abortion*
>
> *Due to yesterday's abortion,*
>
> *Looking forward to seeing you both!*

The last time I left my flat, I was pregnant. I walk to the super-market and think about everything I did and said when I was pregnant. The last time I saw [----], I was pregnant. The last time I spoke to [----], I was pregnant.

I am wearing a heavy coat with the hood up. I gradually real-ise that people can tell I've had an abortion just by looking at me. I feel like I'm on my first spacewalk. I focus on the edge of the pavement and try to keep moving. Panting, light-headed. I strain to keep my eyes open. I'm going to throw up or shit myself.

I stop on a bench and stare at the entrance to the supermar-ket. I check my phone to see if [----] and [----] have cancelled.

The shopping basket fills until I can barely lift it. I retrace my steps, carefully sliding things back onto shelves. I slope home.

I drag a chair from the living room to the kitchen and survey the results on the counter: shower gel, onions, sushi rice, unscented sanitary pads, bleach, spaghetti hoops, coffee, toilet roll. I check the cupboard again. I find some pasta sauce in the freezer.

I wedge a hot water bottle down the back of my trousers and sit, tiptoed, with the chopping board on my knees. Everything rolls off. I shuffle the chair to the hob and burn my wrist on the lip of the pan. I drop the wooden spoon and red spatters up the wall.

Stand under the shower again.

Put a dress on and set the table and then get into bed and cry and wait for [----] and [----] to arrive.

What are you crying for? It's done.

'The biological evidence, you know, the hard, er, scientific evidence, tells us that life begins at conception.' 'No, I'm sorry, I can't let you –' 'It's true! This is the evidence. We can we can *see* the baby growing! We can *see* it developing!' 'But it's *not* a baby.' 'Yes it is. Yes yes it is.' 'The language you're using, the language –' 'This isn't about language! The foetus, or or the baby, or whatever you want to call it – is a living human being. Any attempt, *any attempt* to deny that –' 'But the language you're using is designed to –' 'This is about human life! Human life that you would, er, extinguish, just because it's – it's inconvenient.' 'No, no, that's not the point I'm trying to make. My point is –' 'Well, what is your point? So far, you've you've –' 'you're asking the wrong question! This isn't –' 'Is the unborn child a person? *Why* can't you answer that?' 'Why are you calling it an "unborn child"? Why not an "embryo" or a "foetus"? Can't you see –' 'Well hang on, hang on. You're accusing *me* of of being er er manipulative, of using words to, you know, manipulate the argument, but *you're* the one – *you're the one* calling it an *embryo*. It's a human –' 'I'm calling it an embryo because it *is* an embryo! How can you –' 'The medical profession agrees, they *agree*' 'not see the difference!' 'that life begins' 'I think you're overstating' 'at conception! This is the science! Are you are you seriously suggesting, seriously –' 'You're talking about the *potential* for life, not life itself. We don't –' 'On the seventh day, the heart, er, in some form, starts beating. You cannot –' 'I'm sorry, but –' 'you *cannot deny*' 'that is completely false! It's false! I can't let you – ' 'Let him finish his point, please.' 'I'm talking about the *science* here . . . the facts. And the facts are very clear. From the moment of fertilisation, you have a living human being.' 'You're ignoring the *very important* developmental distinctions between –' 'It is a living human being! *Why* can't you accept that? What what would it take –' 'Look, I'm not going to get trapped in this line of argument here.'

[----] is in the bathroom and [----] is scraping plates at the table and asking me how work is going and what I've been up to and how my family are and I say 'good   I had an abortion yesterday   but I'm completely fine now!'

Twelve stops scraping to adjust the angle of the knife in his hand. I try to recall a single conversation we've had about abortion in the last eight years. He turns to me, wincing his eyes slightly. I don't know what his face means. It never occurred to me that he might be anti-abortion. I defuse the room: 'Let me get dessert!'

When I come back from the kitchen, they are talking in low voices and lightly holding hands across the table. Twelve has told Thirteen. I am holding a tin of peaches and some yoghurt I will pretend I don't know has soured. Twelve gets up and comes back with bowls and spoons and a tin opener.

They are doing their sympathetic faces. I don't want them to pity me.

'It was the right thing to do. It was the only thing to do. I couldn't have had it. I wasn't going to have it.'

The first time it happens, it's an accident: some anti-abortion websites are designed not to look like anti-abortion websites.

The second time, I tell myself I'm just curious.

I close the tab.

I reopen the tab.

Of course I'm pro-abortion. I just had one.

ab abort abortion advice aftercare at 5 weeks at 6 weeks after effects bleeding bill clinic cost counselling definition documentary depression debate dream meaning doctor experience essay ethics excuses work effects emotions facts film free fee figures guilt grief guidelines guilt and regret helpline history hoover how much health risks how much blood information infection injection jobs jewellery jokes journal articles kit keepsakes legal laws meaning methods mumsnet movie mod months near me news nsfw numbers operation on trial on demand or adoption or termination pill process procedure pill cost pain prices private cost pills over the counter period poems quotes quiz question questionnaire questions and answers questions to ask rights rates risks rules recovery reviews statistics support network surgery side effects support services services near me suction sign language timeline types tattoo treatment technique trauma tools time limits under 16 under general anaesthetic ultrasound vines vs adoption vs miscarriage via suction vacuum aspiration walk in clinic what to expect window what is it

Fifteen more minutes. Forty-five more minutes.

One website gives way to another website, which gives way to another website, which gives way to another website.

Over sixty million abortions have been performed in the US since Roe v. Wade.

78% of women regret their abortion.

Flavour enhancers are made from the cloned kidney cells of aborted foetuses.

85% of people who have an abortion are single.

Early medical abortion is reversible.

Six hundred thousand girls are terminated every single day.

Nineteen million abortions have been carried out since the introduction of the Abortion Act.

Over the past forty years, fifty-five million children have been murdered by abortion.

Every 1.6 seconds, a baby is aborted.

43% of yearly deaths worldwide are from abortion.

ab abort abortion is barbaric issues abortionist abortionist's salary abortionists caught failing jokes is healthcare
t-shirt is not healthcare is not the answer is not normal
is not the only answer is not family planning is murder-
ing is murder is more dangerous than childbirth is prolife
is population control is painful for the baby is it painful
for the baby protest protests near me protests now is sad
is safe is safe until how many weeks is sick is termination
is termination is women's rights is wrong quotes

Twelve and Thirteen tell me to come over after work. I knock on their door and let myself in. They're stood together in the middle of the living room, like they're about to break some very bad news. Twelve hugs me and I start crying. I think about all the stupid things he's seen me do. This is the stupidest, I decide. I want to apologise.

Why have you done this to yourself?

Thirteen asks what I've eaten today and reappears with a miniature bar of chocolate, fresh from the fridge. I sit on the sofa and munch it quietly, wiping my face on the back of my hand. They give me another.

Why do you rely on people like this?

Twelve has his concerned face on. I ask him if abortion causes autism. He pauses for a moment and I can see him running the scenario.

'OK. If I eat this banana,' he gestures towards the fruit bowl on the table, 'and then I walk out into the road and get hit by a bus – did the banana cause me to get hit by a bus?'

It could have done, I think. What if you had an allergic reaction to the banana? What if the banana was poisoned? What if you dropped the banana peel in the middle of the road, slipped over, and got hit by the bus?

He waits for my response. I nod very slowly, like I understand.

The sliding door to the balcony is kept open. TWELVE and THIRTEEN have positioned themselves so they can see me standing out here, though they are pretending not to look.

Warm, thick air is funnelled up the side of the apartment building. I can smell my hair in the updraught. The sun is setting on the other side of the city. TWELVE asks if I want to help with dinner.

He takes out a pack of steaks from a shopping bag on the floor.

'How do you want it?'

I sit at the table and watch. Smoke hangs around the ceiling lights. He tilts the pan to show me how rare it is.

'Are you sure?'

I cover the whole thing in a thick layer of English mustard and salt and eat it quickly. TWELVE and THIRTEEN tell me they'll eat later.

After dinner, I am expressionless on the sofa. I close my eyes for one second. I am tucked in with a blanket. The fridge opens and closes. Plates are stacked. THIRTEEN's bare feet stick and unstick across the floor. Someone says the word 'counselling'. The volume on the television is turned down. The balcony door is pulled to.

'What you're suggesting is absolutely *appalling*.' 'I'm – I'm try-ing to show –' 'You're seriously comparing an unborn child, an *unborn child*, to a kidney?' 'But you're not –' 'That is one of the most –' 'I didn't say that, [----].' 'I'm completely disgusted, *disgusted*, by this line of argument. It's –' 'That's not –' 'it's an abhorrent comparison, really.' 'Let her answer.' 'Thank you . . . I'm not suggesting that the foetus is, er, an organ, or –' 'I – I'm appalled that you would say this!' 'Let her respond, please.' 'The point of the analogy, [----], is that we would think it wrong to force someone to undergo, er, a serious medical procedure, like donating their kidney, against their will, so –' 'This is utter nonsense!' '*so* – so we should think it wrong, we should think it *wrong*, to force a woman to continue a preg-nancy and deliver a baby against her will!' 'Well, *I'm sorry*, but unfortunately there are consequences –' 'That's unfair.' 'In the real world, one must live with the consequences of one's actions! Using these kinds of of warped ideas to justify –' 'OK let's hear from our next panellist, please.'

The woman sitting next to me on the bus takes a small sandwich bag out of her coat pocket and silently vomits into it repeatedly. Her back arches in a wave. The bag slowly fills up. She ties a knot in the top and drops it neatly into her handbag.

There is an anti-abortion demonstration outside the building where I work. Two people are holding a banner with a faded photograph of a bloody, mangled baby. The monstrous baby is the size of a shopping trolley.

LOVE THEM BOTH

PRO-WOMAN   PRO-BABY   PRO-LIFE

YOUR BABY HAS RIGHTS TOO!!

KILL ME NOW, IT'S MURDER   KILL ME BEFORE BIRTH, IT'S ABORTION

ABORTION KILLS BABIES

There are battery-powered candles and tiny figurines that look like shrimp. I walk past the demonstrators carefully, turning at the last second to make eye contact with a water-damaged photograph of a newborn.

'Is there really? How *awful*,' I hear myself saying, when a colleague asks if I saw the demonstration. 'We should complain to someone.'

A rotten orange is folding in on itself on top of the microwave in the communal kitchen. I poke at it with the end of a pen while I wait for my lunch to heat through.

'I want to um take up this point about ground C – the exemption under which ninety-eight per cent of terminations in the UK are carried out.' 'Sure.' 'Now, ground C permits a termination in instances where the um . . . the *pregnancy* has not exceeded its twenty-fourth week –' 'That's correct.' 'And and I'm quoting here, "the continuance of the pregnancy would involve risk, *greater* than if the pregnancy were terminated, of injury to the physical or mental health of the pregnant woman." Correct?' 'Yes.' 'Now, I'm sure we both have some idea of the um . . . physical complications and dangers that women face during pregnancy and childbirth – and these are are very real, of course – but it's this point about *mental health* that I want to push you on.' 'I think you're overcomplicating the –' 'Well, I'm just I'm just quoting the exemption. This is what it says.' 'Sure.' 'And so I want to put it to you that under the terms of ground C, *anything goes*, because the woman can always claim that it's necessary for her mental health to have a termination.' 'You seem to have forgotten that this is a process that's overseen by medical professionals.' 'No, I'm –' '*Two* doctors have to agree that the abortion is the right course of action. Do you know of any other –' 'Yes but –' 'The woman *doesn't* get to make the choice on her own – and and actually *this* is the problem with abortion law in the UK, in my eyes – her decision is is is overseen, it's always in consultation.' 'Well let's set that aside –' 'I just don't see this distinction you're trying to make –' 'I'm quoting –' 'What are you suggesting a woman do or say to be allowed to have an abortion?'

'I'm simply highlighting a potential issue here, which is that a woman may um . . . present herself to her doctor for an abortion under the terms of ground C –' 'Women *don't* –' 'And actually, *actually*, she wants to abort the baby because it's the wrong sex, for example, or it has the wrong colour eyes, and so on. So –' 'There's very little evidence to suggest –' 'And so what we have, under current legislation, is de facto abortion on demand.'

I dedicate my evenings to finding new anti-abortion campaign groups, charities, discussion boards, and memes.

I save the ones that upset me the most. Ten minutes and four hours later, I am scrolling admiringly through my photo album and it is time to go to work again.

girl   bathroom   pregnancy test   hand pressed against her
head   mouth open   panic   *FUCK, MY MOM IS GONNA*
KILL ME   /   red string   a vein   an umbilical cord   a heart
a dot   a foot with five toes   an embryo in space   *FUCK, MY*
MOM IS GONNA KILL ME

same girl   same bathroom   same pregnancy test   camera one
step back   forehead wrinkled   disgust   *WHAT A PREGNANT*
TEEN THINKS: MY MOM IS GONNA KILL ME   /   a bloody
clump   a ball of something   a mess   a mistake   one blue
vein   *WHAT A FETUS THINKS: MY MOM IS GONNA KILL*
ME

FOURTEEN tells me he's 'sorry to hear that'.

FIFTEEN says he's also having a hard time at the moment, then tells me he'll apologise 'if that's what you want'.

SIXTEEN complains about a urinary tract infection (the doctor says that she can't have sex for a week!) and then says she's surprised I even told her, because she didn't think we were really friends anymore.

I contact human resources to request 'a period of absence'. The form instructs me to describe, 'in as much detail as possible', the reasons why I should be granted leave.

YOU MUST ALSO ATTACH ANY ADDITIONAL SUP-PORTING EVIDENCE.

I ask for written confirmation that the application will not appear on my permanent record, and that the paperwork will be destroyed once it's been reviewed by the board.

The clinic doesn't list a direct telephone number and I've torn up everything in the pick 'n' mix bag. I call the charity who manage the clinic, but the person at the other end isn't able to help. They give me the email address of someone at head office.

I spend a long time working on the email:

> *I would like to have access to my medical records*
>
> *I would like my records from the clinic to be released*
>
> *I am looking to obtain a copy of the clinic's records pertaining to*

I include the dates of the three appointments and the address of the clinic.

I receive a form to complete.

The doctor asks why the abortion isn't on my medical record. I explain that the clinic gave me a choice and, for reasons, I decided for it not to be.

'Will you write the letter or not?'

I list my symptoms: back pain, cramping, heavy bleeding, dizziness, difficulty sleeping, feelings of guilt, lack of appetite, guilt, trouble concentrating, uncontrollable rage, fury, an obsession with pro-life memes, headaches, 'low mood', ringing in my ears, tiredness, shortness of breath.

'I'm actually fine though!' I insist, scrunching my fists.

She tells me that I may wish to consider having some counselling ('absolutely!') and agrees to write the letter in support of my application. I arrange to pick it up from the surgery the next day.

I delete the clinic's request form. I attach the doctor's letter to my leave application.

In a large text box on the front page of the form, I quickly print:

I HAD AN ABORTION A WEEK AGO AND AM STRUGGLING WITH FEELINGS OF GUILT AND SHAME.

At the start of the meeting, I present the paperwork to the line manager for his signature. We are both embarrassed.

The forms are submitted to the administrator.

29 July 2017

I am granted two weeks' leave.

The board have asked me to make you aware that this has been granted in exceptional circumstances, as normally leave requests for a person in your position are rejected.

Please note that no further leave can be granted on these grounds.

Seventeen: administrator.

Eighteen: doctor.

Nineteen: line manager.

Twenty, twenty-one, twenty-two: three board members.

I tell myself to relax. I tell myself to get a fucking grip.

I watch a video of ping-pong trick shots.

I watch a video of a chick hatching from a supermarket egg.

I watch a video of a family of ducks crossing a busy road.

I watch a video of a man making a pancake. He cracks an egg and a chick drops onto the hotplate. He cracks another, same again. He repeats this, three or four times.

I watch a video of someone claiming to be a former abortion clinic worker.

'One of the things that you had shared in a previous interview, [----], was you spent some time working in the "POC" room. Can you share more about your experience in that room and what that room is?' 'Um, "POC" stands for "Products of Conception". In that room, the doctor er when he got through with the abortion procedure, he would walk in there – with the dirty instruments in one hand that he had used for the procedure and in his arm he had a big jar – about this tall – and he had it tucked in his arm – like this. And he would come in there and he would lay down the dirty instruments at the sink and he would take the jar that had the products of conception – as they called it – he would pour it into a giant, er, sifter – kind of like what you would use like for flour – he would pour that out, he would sift through it with his hands, checking for the parts to make sure they were all there.' 'And you'd be standing there watching him doing this?' 'Yes. Sometimes I just . . . couldn't take it. And I would run to the restroom, or run out in the hallway, maybe, and get some supplies or something, just to step out of there for a little while, while he was sifting through that. There was one doctor that would sit there and he would sometimes talk – to *this* – saying – I'll – I'll never forget him saying "now *where's* your little arm? I didn't see your – I'm missing this arm" and he would sift through it, trying to find the pieces and then he'd say – I remember him saying – "Oh *there you are*, now *where's* the head? *Where's* this?"'

I call THREE again.

'I know I'm disgusting.'

'What are you talking about?'

I cry into the phone.

'You're just saying this because of how I reacted. I'm sorry –'

'No. I'm saying it because that's what I think!'

I'm walking through a busy shopping centre. I don't know why I'm here. Tears drip down my chin.

'Where are you?'

'I *deserve* to feel like this!'

I'm shouting now.

'And it's fine! Because I deserve it! Because it's my fault for being stupid and disgusting enough to get pregnant in the first place!'

It doesn't matter what day it is. I mute my phone and get into bed.

I shut my eyes and cross-reference all the news articles and police statements and coroners' reports I've read. I am working the case.

According to local police, the baby girl was abandoned in the woods in the early hours of Sunday morning 'next to an old tip' The prosecution described to the court how the woman 'threw the infant child into the septic tank' 'It was not a simple task; it required significant planning and effort' The woman claims that the three-month-old foetus was already dead when she attempted to dispose of it The woman is reported to have died following a misguided attempt to self-induce a miscarriage Her internet search history revealed a series of searches on how to abort a pregnancy The woman was found by police following a welfare check The coroner's inquest heard how the woman ingested half a litre of apple cider vinegar

I read hundreds of testimonies from people claiming to be former abortion clinic workers.

'you know foetuses can't scream, right? My god – if they could' Pictures of abortion clinics 'I finally broke down and realised that I couldn't stand looking at those tiny bodies anymore' Pictures of abortion tools 'what they don't want you to know is that three or four babys a day are born alive during abortion procedures' Pictures: 6 weeks 'the doctor sticks his fingers down the baby's throat' Pictures: 5 weeks 'he seemed to especially enjoy aborting the little baby girls'

It doesn't matter what's real. I know that I won't be able to unsee that   or that   or that   but I keep scrolling.

The embryo is now around 4 millimetres and resembles an orange pip   Your baby is now 9 millimetres long, or around the size of a fingernail   The heart is rapidly developing and will start beating soon   Just eighteen days from conception, your baby's heart begins to beat with its own blood supply blood flows through baby's veins   At six weeks, your baby has a heartbeat

I stop when my eyes hurt. I clear my search history and cache again, then I clean the keyboard and laptop screen. I get into bed.

When questioned by police, the woman claimed that she had 'put him in a bin' CCTV from a local restaurant showed the woman placing the nine-week-old foetus in a city-centre bin in the early hours of Friday morning Detective Inspector [----] told the court that the woman had repeatedly lied to police officers throughout the 'extremely distressing' case, admitting her involvement only when video evidence was retrieved Her internet search history revealed a series of attempts to purchase the drugs typically used in a medical abortion, mifepristone and misoprostol

An old flatmate once accidentally switched off the freezer when we both went away for a few weeks. After some beers at the train station with his friends, the flatmate came home and opened the front door. The flat was heavy with the smell of rancid meat: ammonia, vinegar, rotten eggs. The flatmate managed to enlist two friends, who were still out drinking nearby, to help him try to clean out the freezer before I came home. They found a pair of rubber gloves underneath the sink and each set up a processing station: scooping (left glove), bagging, bleaching (right glove). Beef mince pouring out of its exploded packet. Pork sausage blossoming from its casing. Disintegrated fish finger box with a distinctive blue aura. Unrecognisable matter. They took it in turns to crane their heads out the window and retch in the corridor outside the flat. One was drunk enough he could continue on in these rest breaks, spooning the rotten food out from the freezer drawers with his bare hands.

I imagine this material, triple-bagged, in the communal bins outside the building. The bag gently expands.

I picture Two in his flat. I imagine him crying. I imagine him cleaning out the wheelie bin. It's his turn to do it.

I don't want him to be a part of this, so I invent a man to occupy myself with. It doesn't matter who he is.

I imagine him showering. I imagine him getting knocked off his bike.

I dress him. I brush his hair. I conjure up a link between our present conditions. Something is ruining his life, but he is incapable of understanding what it is.

He wakes up with a start. Choking. Gasping. Something rush-
ing up his throat and down the sides of his face. He reaches
for the bedside lamp. Coughing. Fumbling in the dark for his
phone. His pyjama trousers feel hot. A flatmate appears. Get
out! *He pulls the covers away. His legs are shaking.* Get out! *The*
flatmate runs to get the washing up bowl. This is it. He tries to
sit up straight, but his stomach heaves again. Gasping. He leans
forward and slides his fingers into his mouth. His bowels squeeze.
His oesophagus expands and contracts. He feels it leave him.
Coughing. Straining. Saliva pools on the mattress. He observes
the hot jelly. Spits. The flatmate turns on the bedroom light.

I nearly walk in front of a bus. I nearly cut my hair off. I nearly tell my family. I nearly buy a Stanley knife. I nearly wipe my hard drive. I nearly go to the local church. I nearly walk up the car ramp of the multi-storey. I nearly quit my job.

I'm minding my own business, doing nothing, and then I'm drooling and grunting and pulling my hair and punching my ankles. I fold in half on the sofa and knock my head between my knees.

I'm still for a minute. The blood in my neck makes my head twitch.

I say something entirely pathetic and meaningless, to no one, like: 'If you don't stop now, it'll take over your life.'

I contact the free counselling service at work. There is an appointment available later that morning.

More paperwork, though this time I don't care what happens to it.

Nearly every day I have taken little interest or pleasure in doing things   Nearly every day I have felt down, depressed, or hopeless   Nearly every day I have had trouble falling or staying asleep or sleeping too much   Nearly every day I have felt tired or had little energy   Nearly every day I have felt desperate or as though I had no options   Nearly every day I have felt embarrassed or ashamed   Nearly every day I have felt bad about myself, or that I am a failure, or that I have let myself or my family down   Nearly every day I have had difficulty concentrating on things, such as reading the newspaper or watching television   Nearly every day I have felt feelings of guilt, shame, or embarrassment   Nearly every day I have had thoughts about harming myself or others   Nearly every day I have made plans to end my life   Nearly every day I have felt nervous or anxious   Nearly every day I have had trouble relaxing   Nearly every day I have been so restless that it is hard to sit still   Nearly every day I have been bothered by becoming easily annoyed or irritable   Nearly every day I have felt afraid, as if something awful might happen

I spend the fifty-minute session staring at a discoloured print of a red daisy. The daisy is roughly the same size as the counsellor's head.

When she invites me to say the word 'shame' – to confess to her that 'I feel ashamed' – my top lip lifts into a snarl, like I'm trying to smile or suppress a laugh. I tell myself it's a trapped nerve.

I describe the websites and memes and hashtags and message boards.

'Maybe I'm secretly anti-abortion,' I say.

'Do you think some of this material you've been looking at online has changed how you feel?'

'You want me to say *yes*.'

She says nothing.

'But maybe this is what I've always thought, and I just didn't know I thought it.'

'That seems like a rather complicated explanation.'

I say nothing.

The counsellor watches as I perform my routine:

I am disgusting   my body is disgusting   my behaviour was disgusting   I shouldn't have gotten pregnant   it is disgusting

I allowed myself to be pregnant   being pregnant was disgusting
the pregnancy was disgusting   I shouldn't have continued the
pregnancy   I shouldn't have told anyone about the abortion
I shouldn't have had the abortion

After the session, I get out onto the street and start laughing
uncontrollably. I take out my phone and hold it to my ear and
talk at it.

The can of Swedish surströmming in the back of the fridge has begun to bulge and take shape. It has been causing him concern for several weeks. He routinely takes the can out to inspect it, noting new spots of rust around the rim. Due to the complicated process of opening the tin (it should be submerged in a bucket of water and pierced at a forty-five-degree angle) and preparing the fish (which must be washed, gutted, filleted, and checked for roe), he knows he'll never taste the fermented herring. It's probably disgusting anyway.

He wraps the can in a black sack and abandons it in the outside bin.

I pace around the living room and punch my hips. I hit myself repeatedly over the head with a book. I gnash my teeth and bite down on my tongue. I think about shutting my fingers inside the door. The window mechanism. Forcing my hands into a pan of boiling water. The bottom of the blender.

'You had an appointment with your counsellor yesterday, didn't you?' the receptionist asks.

'Yes.'

'We don't usually do appointments this close together – since you had one yesterday. This is a free service and normally we're simply too busy to arrange appointments this soon after your last one. When we have a busy period, you won't be able to see your counsellor this soon after your last appointment, because you saw her recently – yesterday, in fact. Usually, it takes a few weeks.'

'OK, it doesn't matter then.'

'Well, on this occasion, the counsellor is free and can see you today at either one o'clock or three o'clock. This is a one-off, though.'

She wants me to thank her; I tell her I don't want the appointment.

'This time, there is a slot available for you – so it's fine.'

'No – I've changed my mind; I don't need an appointment. I'm sorry for wasting your time.'

I go to hang up and hear her shout 'wait!'

She puts me on hold.

'Your counsellor is looking forward to seeing you, which appointment would you like: one o'clock or three o'clock?'

I recognise the tone. I have behaved like a brat. I flap my free arm against my side and try to steady my voice.

'Thanks, but I've told you. I don't want the appointment. I've changed my mind.'

'*Look*,' her register lowers like she's leaning into the handset, 'I'm sorry, I didn't know your circumstances before, but I've spoken to your counsellor and she's agreed to see you, and I'm going to get in trouble now if you don't take this appointment.'

Counsellor and receptionist: Twenty-three, twenty-four.

'I deserve to be punished for getting pregnant in the first place. The abortion is a punishment for putting myself in that position.'

'Would you tell a friend whose morning-after pill had failed that they deserved to be punished? Would you tell them that it was their fault for getting pregnant?'

'No, but that's not how it works. That's not a useful way to live your life.'

'So you're saying that the abortion was the right thing to do – *and* it was a punishment?'

'Yes.'

'Can it be both?'

'Yes: I shouldn't have gotten pregnant, and I shouldn't have had the abortion. The abortion doesn't correct or excuse the mistake in the first place.'

'But it *was* a mistake. Are we not all allowed to make mistakes sometimes?'

'No, not like this.'

'What would it take for you to forgive yourself for –'

'I had to do it, because I didn't want to have a *baby*' (it's like I'm saying the word for the first time) 'but it was disgusting and wrong.'

'Tell me again about these websites that you've been looking at.'

The men in the backroom of the phone repair shop paw through my photo albums, browser history, recently deleted items, incognito tabs.

#prolife #prolifearmy pelvic inflammation symptoms *You Won't Believe This 4D Scan of What Unborn Babies Do in The Womb* can babies cry in the womb do babies cry in the womb *FUCK, MY MOM IS GONNA KILL ME FUCK, MY MOM IS GONNA KILL ME MY MOM IS GONNA KILL ME!* week 6 pregnancy six week pregnant 3 weeks pregnant #babieslivesmatter *Here's Your Baby Fruit Size Chart* #abortionkills #abortionismurder #endabortion

'Oh those! Oh god, those those! Yeah, *those* Yeah, sorry Oh, they're not mine God, sorry! Yeah, sorry they're a bit weird.'

'They're not mine,' I practise to myself, over and over, on the walk back to the shop.

I know I need to stop, but I can't.

He throws himself at the low sofa in the hotel lobby. He tries to cross his legs, but his hips are at the wrong angle. On the glass table in front of him is an extravagant display of fruit. He leans forward, feeling his trousers tighten around his thighs, and discreetly examines the underside of a tangerine. A glossy black beetle crawls out from the display. He puts the tangerine back.

3:52 a.m. A surge of adrenaline. Someone is outside his bedroom door. No, they aren't. He pulls the covers up to his neck. Something is walking across his face. No, it isn't. Something is burrowing inside his ear canal. He swipes at his hair. Rustling, crunching. He grabs his phone and shines the screen over the bed. They are everywhere. Pulverised under his body. Mangled in the sheets. Hundreds of the things. Hundreds more dead.

My counsellor's head is crowned with red petals. It is our third and final session. I take extra care not to mention anything that might reveal it's my birthday.

'I shouldn't be this upset about it,' I say. 'I'm not allowed to be this upset.'

I stop myself from crying. I want to show progression.

'It's like smashing a glass because you want to smash a glass, and then being upset and angry that you've smashed the glass,' I decide.

It occurs to me for a second that this is, in fact, quite reasonable. I trail off.

'It sounds like, from our previous conversations, that even though you didn't want to continue the pregnancy, you still feel it as a loss.'

I nod and nod and nod and try not to cry.

'And it's OK to feel it as a loss. To feel conflicted.'

The arc of my nod is huge now, like I'm miming my understanding.

'Oh, and happy birthday,' she says as I leave.

I call TEN. When he answers, I apologise for calling and hang up.

I punch my temples and hold a sofa cushion over my face and scream and cry and pinch the skin under my thighs and slap my hands together and thunder the balls of my feet on the floor.

Are you finished?

I put myself in front of some screens for a few hours to calm down.

Eventually, I am placid enough to have dinner with TWELVE and THIRTEEN. When I arrive at their flat, I am presented with flowers and truffles. They are indulging me. I should be grateful. I want the day to be over. TWELVE opens a bottle of acidic non-alcoholic wine. We all individually remark on how light and fruity and refreshing it is, how we should get it again sometime.

No blood for twenty-four hours.

I go on a short spacewalk, bending my knees with each step to cushion the impact. Waiting at the crossing, I feel a hot spurt. I tie my shirt around my waist and skulk home.

I throw my bottom half in the washing machine. Dripping over the toilet, I scrunch up some paper and blot between my legs. The blood is insides red.

MY MOM IS GONNA KILL ME!   red sponge   petroleum jelly   count the fingers again   it's not real   it can't be real   'Don't look in the toilet bowl. Just flush.'

I decide, on the basis of absolutely no medical advice, that I should wait until there are five consecutive days of nonbleeding before I can consider it 'over'.

The queue is moving again. He shifts his weight from foot to foot in time to the music. The girl in front is sweeping her hand along the bottom of her bag. She takes out a compact mirror, licks her middle finger, and runs it close to the eyelashes under each eye. Everyone steps forward. He admires the damp line down the back of her dress. He thinks about touching her. Everyone steps forward. The taps have stopped running. Someone is working their way down the row of alcohol-gel dispensers, pressing down harder on the hinge each time. Nothing. Everyone steps forward. Everyone steps forward.

He locks the door and unbuttons his jeans. The lights cut out. Shouting. Whooping. The lights come on. He jumps back into the door. Dark water spills over the rim and onto the floor.

I take the pregnancy test given to me by the clinic. I watch it develop so I don't miss anything.

Negative.

I buy two more and take those.

Negative.

Negative.

The bleeding has stopped.

The late-night searches taper off. I delete the photographs, newspaper reports, journal articles, and memes, then I take them out of the bin and move them into a new folder called 'research'.

I tell TWENTY-FIVE to TWENTY-SEVEN in the same night.

TWENTY-SIX tells me he could never get one. 'That's understandable,' I say.

[----] messages to ask how it's going and I reply: 'Pretty bad. I had an abortion last month.'

Twenty-eight.

It is someone's birthday. I'm already late. I take off the jeans and put tights and a skirt on. I take off the skirt and put a dress on. I take off the dress and put a different dress on. I take off the tights and put a different pair of tights on. I take off the tights and put shoes on. I take off the dress and put a different dress on. I take off the dress and put jeans on. I take off the jeans and put tights and a dress on.

A few drinks in, I want to show TWENTY-SEVEN something on my phone. She leans over.

bloody mucus on a dime

weeping stone angel

surgical scissors

I try not to acknowledge the panic in my body, but I can feel my head shaking. I scroll past the images.

The man I've been watching all night (*disgusting, look at him*) walks in slow motion towards me. Pull the pig. He asks what my name is. I think carefully about what my lips are doing. His eyes narrow, like he's considering a complex moral issue. I want to run my fingernails across his dirty scalp. I don't want him to touch me. We look at each other.

I go to the toilets to check my make-up. I close the cubicle door and tuck my dress under my chin. I want him to touch me. Blood has soaked through my underwear and tights. The insides of my thighs are rubbed pink.

This is what you get.

I squeeze a piece of toilet tissue around my underwear and down my drink. I open the cubicle door and strut past the queue for the toilets, past TWENTY-SEVEN and my friends, past the man, and home.

The two smaller blisters on his foot have been absorbed by a new, superior blister. He forces the liquid around, examining its limits. His experiment reveals a cluster of black dots, deep under the skin. He manipulates the blister to get a better look. Something is living in there. He wrenches the foot into the light. Something is definitely in there. The blister is even bigger now. He pinches the skin until it splits. The liquid drains.

Another wedding. I haven't exercised since the abortion and I feel dumpy.

No one will be looking at you.

I miss the first train on the way to the venue, so I stand on the platform, gripping the slit in my dress.

No one will ever look at you.

My bag slips off my shoulder and explodes on the floor. I stuff a fistful of sanitary towels, tampons, and confetti into the bag. The train arrives and I skid gracelessly into the carriage. I hold on to the rail and let go of the dress. I wish I could see my phone. I get off at the wrong stop and totter to the quiet end of the platform.

When I reach the right station, I miss the sign for the lift and stop halfway up the stairs to pant, pretending to check my messages. Sweat runs behind my ears.

I stand up for the bride and check my seat for blood.

I spend the day thinking about the absorbent pads in the underarms of my dress, the body tape slowly peeling off my chest, the damp sanitary pad, folded over the edges of my 'invisible' underwear.

I tell TWENTY-NINE, THIRTY, THIRTY-ONE, and THIRTY-TWO at the reception.

THIRTY-TWO holds my hand and cries on the way back from the off licence.

THIRTY-ONE's friend asks for my phone number, then doesn't reply to my message.

THIRTY-ONE told him, I decide.

No blood for eleven days.

I catch up with work. I clean the bathroom. I trim my bikini line and go swimming. I make ravioli. I go to the pub and get drunk instantly and joke that I never want to have sex again. Everybody laughs.

The conversations around me return to normal.

They thought it was appendicitis How can you *not know* after two months?   Emergency contraception isn't contraception Did you not use any protection?   Did you know you can bulk buy pregnancy tests on the internet and they're cheaper than in the shops because they don't have the plastic casing?   I've taken the morning-after pill twice   I've had the morning-after pill about five times   I had to get the morning-after pill last week   No, but he bought me a coffee afterwards   You could have caught anything Have you been tested? I would get tested twice, just to be sure   Did you know that [----] had one?   that's why she moved away   You can catch AIDS I knew a girl at university who didn't know how to use a condom   She didn't know how to put one on! So many women today don't know how to use contraception properly   Sex education should be taught in the home, not at school   How pregnant were you?   Did you come?   Did he break up with her?   She said that she felt nothing   How many times have you taken the morning-after pill?   I've never used contraception   I keep a thermometer by my bed   My ex-girlfriend had one   My old housemate had one   [----] had one   Would you breastfeed?   Have you joined a union?   I shouldn't be telling you this, but [----]'s best friend, [----], had one   I haven't seen her since   I took her to the clinic   it started on the way home   I've never told anyone that   Everyone says the condom broke   no one says they didn't use one

I have a period, I think, but it's difficult to tell. I add it to the growing evidence to support my no longer being pregnant.

I know that the period is supposed to be a sign that I'm in good working order, but I continue to treat my body with suspicion.

I imagine that the cervix is still 'prepared', 'dilated', 'ripe'.

I imagine losing a tampon. I imagine losing a hand.

I never want to be pregnant again.

I compare the failure rates and side-effects of the contraception I haven't already tried and decide on an 'intrauterine system': the hormonal coil.

The T-shaped piece of plastic will continuously release a synthetic progesterone, called levonorgestrel, into the uterus. The coil will thicken the cervical mucus and thin the lining of the uterus, though the manufacturer explains that 'it is not known exactly how these actions work together to prevent pregnancy'.

I sit with my hands in my lap, like a princess, and wait for the doctor to speak. I have worn leather shoes and a tailored jacket and a neutral lipstick.

'I'd like to have the hormonal coil fitted – please.'

'Right –'

'I've been thinking about it for some time, and I've tried two different contraceptive pills and the implant, and I think that the hormonal coil is right for me.'

I'm immediately convinced he'll say no. Can he say no? What do I do if he says no?

'OK.'

During the consultation, I tell the doctor I had an abortion two months ago. He turns to look at the computer screen.

'Why isn't it on your medical records?' he asks. 'Couldn't you have just had this done while you were in there?'

Thirty-three.

I wear two condoms and pull out before I come   My girl-friend said that your period stops underwater   I'm so scared of getting someone pregnant   She told me she had the contra-ceptive implant, but how do I know if she actually did?   I can't believe I never got you pregnant   I can't believe you think I'm capable of that   Did you *tell* him not to come?   Have you tried the rhythm method?   If I was a woman, I'd get an abortion tomorrow!   Contraception is a luxury, not a right   Maybe if you really want to not get pregnant again you should use the coil *and* the pill   it's obviously completely up to you though If I was a woman, I'd get an IED   Some people shouldn't be allowed to have sex   It was falling off so I took it off   I thought you said it was fine   It was too tight so I took it off   They're uncomfortable   Can you put it on for me?   I want to be able to feel you   How far along were you?   I completely respect what you're saying, but I just don't like wearing a condom Was it a one-night stand?   I understand why you did it, in your situation, but personally I don't think that it's right   Did you tell The Father?   But we're already basically having sex   I didn't hear you   Just for a second, I promise

For reasons that have not been explained, I have to order the coil myself at the pharmacy, then bring it to the appointment for the doctor to insert. BYO medical equipment.

The pharmacist looks at the prescription and returns with a ten-inch-long box. I laugh.

'Do you want a bag to put it in?'

In the waiting room, I see [----]. We telepathically agree not to acknowledge each other. There's no reception in the surgery, but we stare at our phones anyway. I scroll through my missed calls. When his name is announced, I start typing a random string of numbers into the calculator. He walks past.

The bed whirring higher. I am breathing in through my nose. I am smoothing the hem of my shirt. I am breathing out through my mouth.

'Knees apart and heels tucked underneath your bottom.'

I imagine her recoiling when I part my legs. Calling another doctor in.

Her hand on the ankle, repositioning the foot. I pull the other heel further in. She moves around the room. The pedal bin opens and closes.

She releases the button. The bed shudders. Then up again. Down again. She adjusts her chair.

'I'm going to examine you now.'

I count the corners of the square ceiling tiles under my breath. It doesn't matter it's four every time.

'I used to count down from ten when I was having my contractions,' she chuckles.

I expel air from my nose in a way that could mean I find that interesting.

'Cough.'

I cough. The device is inserted.

I can feel it inside myself for a few hours and then it disappears.

I bleed continuously for several weeks. I'm back to where I started.

Inside my bag is a smaller secret bag: spare underwear, pads (light and heavy), wet wipes, ibuprofen, paracetamol, co-codamol.

Walking across a large room to give a presentation, I listen to the sanitary pad stick and unstick from the inside of my thigh.

My mum had eight abortions   [----] had one when she was
a teenager   She just had a breakdown in this club we were
in   How could you have been so fucking stupid?   It was like
five years later or something and I was the only person who
had any idea what was going on   Why have you done this to
yourself?   She couldn't stand up   God, I had so much irre-
sponsible sex in my twenties!   but I never got pregnant   We
had to take her home   I don't use contraception, I just hope
he pulls out in time and take a pregnancy test basically every
month   I'm so sorry   When do you count from?   Is [----] the
dad?   I'm sorry   I'm so sorry   It was my fault, I'm sorry   Was
[----] the dad?   I'm sorry I didn't say anything when you told
me   I just didn't know what to say   I'm sorry I said you were
stupid   I'm sorry I said it was your fault   I'm sorry that you
feel that way   I didn't mean for you to be so upset   Sorry,
I don't mean that   Was [----] the baby daddy?   I didn't mean
to say 'baby', sorry   Can I say 'the father'?   'the dad'?   'the man
who got you pregnant'?   Can I say, 'got you pregnant'?   I don't
know why I even said it   Christ, that was a really insensitive
thing to say in front of you, wasn't it?   given what you've been
through, I mean   you know   the ab –

I have cramps for an afternoon, then a day, two days, four days.

Here I am: hanging on to the top of a cubicle door, twisting my hips left to right.

Here I am: sat on the kerb in a side alley, head tucked between my knees, grinding my knuckles into the pavement.

I take painkillers for the pain, and then because I'm worried about the pain, and then because I don't want to worry about worrying about the pain.

You deserve to feel like this.

I ignore the diarrhoea.

This is what you get.

Another wedding. TWENTY-EIGHT has asked me to be his plus one. I arrive at his flat the night before and shave my legs in the bath while he orders pizza. I bob beneath the water and force my belly out, like a little island. I am 6.9 months pregnant.

The boiler clicks on and off. His flatmates laugh in the kitchen. I watch the goosebumps on my breasts. I close my eyes and imagine TWENTY-EIGHT on the other side of the bathroom door. Sitting on the edge of the bath. The tips of his fingers in the water. Steam lifts from my body.

The doorbell rings.

I iron his shirt. I use his towel. I take two ibuprofen and two aspirin and line the corners of my clutch bag with papery sanitary pads, just in case.

We look good together. His flatmates are overexcited. I want him to compliment me. I want him to touch me. I don't want him to touch me.

In the taxi, he asks if I'm alright.

'Of course!' I shout, examining the creases in my dress.

Why are you trying to impress him?

Why are you wearing so much perfume?

Disgusting, really, you only had an abortion five months ago and you're already planning your next.

I am taking in every detail of the buttons on his shirt.

My face says: attentive and interested.

The stitching, the distance apart, the lettering around the edge.

I want to reach across and undo that one, right there.

He stops to ask if I think this will ruin our friendship. I tell him to shut the fuck up.

I am trying to concentrate, but my perspective keeps switching.

I see myself laid out. The inside of my body is like the inside of his mouth. Wet tissue. The white paper sheet winding over the bed. The doctor's hand pushing down on the pubic bone. The plastic seal on the box of disposable gloves. The nurse's fingers.

I observe the scene.

His beard on my neck. His hand around the back of my head.

I go to take a shower but there's no hot water. I fill the bath a few inches and squat over it, scooping water up over myself.

I stand at the end of the bed and try to decide whether or not it was a good idea. My big break.

He sits up on his elbows and tries not to look at my body. I laugh nervously. He looks down then looks away, and I feel a hot stream run down the inside of my leg. I press my legs together and creep to the bathroom in a towel.

He has peeled back the covers and is closely examining several smears of blood in the centre of the bed. I wonder if he might rub my nose in it.

I spend the day watching him experiment with different brands of pre-stain treatment: washing and rewashing, pre-treating and washing, soaking and rinsing.

The sheets hang on the banister while we cook dinner.

'Good night, then?' his flatmate nudges.

My visit to the sexual health clinic marks the start of our relationship.

'Do you have any children?'

'No.'

'And have you ever been pregnant?'

'Yes.'

Sometimes sex is new and exciting; sometimes I'm there while it happens.

When it's good, I'm interrupted by inappropriate or disgusting thoughts.

I tell myself I need to concentrate harder.

girl   bathroom   pregnancy test   hand over nose and mouth
disbelief   *MY MOM IS GONNA KILL ME!* / red translucent
fingers and fingernails   fingers and fingernails   *MY MOM IS
GONNA KILL ME!*

I'm almost always bleeding, or 'spotting' ('what's that?'), or showering, or in pain, or looking for a toilet. I am pre-menstrual, menstrual, post-menstrual.

It's different now he's having sex with me.

If I mention the abortion, TWENTY-EIGHT sits very still and stops talking. He stares at the door. He checks the weather on his phone. Sometimes a full minute will pass.

I stop talking about it.

The jar launches itself from the cupboard and shatters on the floor. It's too late to stop his foot. Bright and sharp, then hot, then wet. He unsticks his foot and lifts it up for inspection. It's impossible to tell how large the piece of glass is. He looks around the floor and tries to mentally piece the jar back together. The foot is dripping now. He remembers an airless afternoon at work spent watching his manager breathe into a dummy. Something about how sometimes you should leave it in. His standing ankle buckles. How it can do more damage on the way out. He grips the piece of glass and looks away.

The doctor explains that the pain and bleeding may or may not be due to the abortion, which could affect my menstrual cycle in any number ways for up to three years, or more.

'The truth is we just don't know.'

I am encouraged to keep a 'pain diary'.

'It feels like a contraction,' I say. The doctor laughs.

'I can assure you that it doesn't.'

I ask for an ultrasound to check the placement of the coil.

'If that's what you want to do.'

He's tired, and he doesn't want you to be upset, and he's not very good at talking about this sort of thing, and he doesn't know what to say, and he's with his friends at the pub, and he's just on his way out, and he can't begin to understand what you've been through, and actually, as a man, wouldn't it be wrong of him to pretend to understand, because he can't, and he doesn't, and last month you *did say* that you were feeling better, and fucking hell can you just *not*, for one second.

The white bulb in the bedside lamp next to his bed. The shape of my body across the room.

I am lying on my back with my legs apart.

His fingers inside me.

The gap in the blinds near the ceiling. The concentric circles in the lamp.

I am lying on my back with my legs apart.

She has inserted the speculum and is placing something on the cervix.

'Have you had an ultrasound before?'

'No.'

The screen is turned away from me.

The abortion never happened.

The ultrasound technician slides the transducer back and forth.

You are eight months pregnant.

He asks if I've drunk the litre of water like I was told to.

'Yes.'

'Go back out to the waiting room and drink some more water.'

I stare at the ceiling.

'Or I'll have to do an internal scan.'

He thinks this sounds threatening. I tell him I would like to have a transvaginal scan now, because it's too painful to hold it any longer.

'Go back out and drink more water.'

He sends me out for thirty minutes.

I watch two other patients come and go. They burst out of his office with their coats and bags and phones and water bottles. My ears are ringing.

The nurse calls me back in. I stand up and piss myself for a second before I can hold it.

He presses down. He presses down harder. I'm in the way again.

'We'll need to do an internal ultrasound.'

I sit up on my elbows and peel off my jeans.

He inserts the probe into the vagina. It pushes against the cervix.

Click. He pulls it down. Click. He pulls it up. Click.

He extracts the probe. I snap my legs shut. The nurse draws the curtain and I get dressed.

'Is the coil in the right place?' I ask.

'You'll need to see your doctor.'

'Can you not just tell me whether it's alright?'

He says nothing.

'Did you not *just see* it on the ultrasound?'

'You'll need to discuss this with your doctor.'

'But can you at least tell me if it's in the right place or not?'

'Call your doctor in a week and arrange an appointment.'

I would have had a baby today.

'The IUS is in the correct position.'

The doctor prescribes mefenamic acid for the pain and tranexamic acid for the irregular bleeding.

'It's really a question of pain management.'

I ask if the pain and spotting and nausea and diarrhoea and bleeding could be endometriosis.

'Could be.'

I wait.

'Though that would just mean referring you to a gynaecologist, then more testing. I'm not sure that's what you want.'

I say nothing on matters relating to changes to abortion legislation, public consultations, ongoing legal battles, high-profile cases, exclusion zones, and so on.

Displaying my new knowledge of these subjects will reveal my secret, I tell myself, which thirty-six people know.

He jerks at his tie. A little hand on the back of his trousers. Laughter. The band kick in. He drifts towards the bouncy castle and slips off his shoes. He clenches and unclenches his jaw. The little hand lets go. Something is pressing down on his chest. The pain is sensational. This is it, he thinks. He places his arms around the turret, like he might give it one last kiss. His legs shake. The generator strains. Warm air courses through the mottled plastic. He is sweating and shivering. The guy rope pops. Someone calls his name from behind the gazebo. He is crying out. He lets go and the turret jumps up. The generator relaxes. He's gone.

The pre-agreed parts of the body are touched in an order perfected through repetition. The waist, the hip, the thigh.

I've killed off my imaginary man and replaced him with an imaginary apartment, somewhere on the Italian coast. The kitchen renovations are nearly complete. Tonight, I'm working on the balcony.

The tide is going out. The curtains shift slightly in the breeze. Perfect. I'll do the bathroom tomorrow.

It is my birthday again and I vow not to make a fuss. My belly gurgles. I am repeatedly asked why the boyfriend isn't here. I wear an expensive silk dress to a bar and my friends sing Happy Birthday so loud strangers join in. I feel myself start to cry and desperately try to read everyone's reactions.

How many people here have you told?

I blink and swallow a lot.

In the bathroom mirror, I mouth a brief congratulatory speech to no one, wincing my face into a smile.

Two days, then four, then seven. Eight. Nine.

I try to see how long it'll take TWENTY-EIGHT to call me, but I cave and scream at him on the way to work.

He says he knows that I'm 'going through something', but he can't help me.

I'm driving through the fog, en route to a group holiday. I don't want to be here, but we've already paid.

'I'm concentrating on keeping us on the road!' I bark, pathetically, when [----] observes that I'm quiet.

When we arrive at the house, I announce that I have a headache so I don't have to explain that I was pregnant so I had an abortion so I had the coil fitted so I have cramps and back pain and diarrhoea and bleeding.

We get the twin room.

The group takes it in turns to cook breakfast.

Today: boiled eggs.

I haven't eaten eggs since the abortion. I can't explain myself, so I don't.

[----] smashes his egg on the edge of the dining table. He takes it over to the sink, rinses it, and eats it whole. He turns and grins. Everyone laughs.

I fight to clear the table first.

Halfway up the idiot mountain, I can tell I've started bleeding again. I walk ahead, imagining the scree giving way behind me.

I think about my beautiful apartment in Italy.

The balcony doors are open. I am setting the table for dinner. A moped zips past. I take out two crystal glasses from the top shelf in the kitchen. My pink satin spaghetti strap slips off my shoulder. Somebody knocks at the door.

Nothing but clouds at the top.

'What was the point in that?' I scoff.

TWENTY-EIGHT walks away. [----] tells me there's no need to be so miserable.

We take photographs together in different combinations and head into the visitor centre.

I pour the water out of my boots and patter in my socks to the toilets, where I bounce the cubicle door off my head. I feel sharp again. I change into dry clothes.

3:52 a.m. The light behind the blinds is finally changing colour. I get up and poke around the kitchen: little piles of tobacco, a half-eaten bag of sweets, group meal smeared around the stove. I check if the car is still there.

When I get back to our room, I slide into TWENTY-EIGHT's bed and kiss his neck and ears. I run my hand up under his shirt. I stroke his hair. His heart shudders through the muscles in his back. He lies very still, like roadkill. I stop and get into my bed.

I am smoothing my legs over my rare and expensive sheets in the imaginary apartment. My dress is in a pile somewhere. The shower turns on.

When TWENTY-EIGHT breaks up with me, I call him every few days to try to renegotiate the terms.

What if I never talk about it again. What if I promise I'll never even think about it again, ever. What if I have some more counselling. What if I call right now and ask for some counselling. What if it didn't happen. What if it never happened.

'Just listen to me for a second,' I snarl down the line, 'just fucking *listen* to me.'

I can't stop myself.

'I need you to understand what I'm saying: You *said* you wouldn't do this.'

He can no longer recall the conversation in question.

In a gesture he hopes I'll interpret as definitive and conclusive, he tells me he was never, 'ever', attracted to me. I respond with the worst thing I can think of.

We are walking through the market together, taking it in turns to stop and point. We are kissing and I am running my fingers along the damp collar of his shirt. Pig leg. Oyster as big as a face. The juicer emits a fine mist. I order something. He twists my wet curl of hair around his fist. When his back is turned, I lean in to cup an enormous blood orange with both hands.

'Quanto costa?' he asks, over my shoulder.

After a night of heavy drinking with THIRTY-FIVE and THIRTY-SIX, we set off home in separate directions. I walk a few steps and think about chips maybe, then stop. I turn back the way I came and walk in the opposite direction from my flat. I don't know what I'm doing.

I keep walking and walking and then I'm standing in the alley behind the abortion clinic, next to two wheelie bins chained to the wall.

I glance up at the security camera. This looks bad. I don't know what I want to do.

A man appears at the entrance to the alley. I try to look like I'm waiting for someone. I take out my phone, unlock it, lock it, and put it back in my bag. I step past the man and walk home.

I've lost control of the list.

Thirty-seven.

THIRTY-EIGHT: who acts like he didn't know, though I know
THIRTY-SEVEN already told him.

Smear test.

'Your cervix is very red.'

'What colour is it supposed to be?'

No answer. The nurse peers inside and tells me that there are several polyps on my cervix.

'Is that bad? Do they need to be removed?'

'They might just go on their own.'

'But how would I know? Do I need to see the doctor?'

'You can if you want.'

The bed moves closer and closer to the ceiling tiles. I imagine being crushed up against them. I have chosen to keep my socks on. The doctor inserts the speculum. It's hard to breathe properly. I know I'll be sick if I exhale fully. I pant politely.

'There are no polyps on your cervix.'

'What?' I look down between my knees at the doctor.

'The nurse must have got it wrong.'

I come up with excuses to be near the clinic. I loop past it at the start and end of my run. I stop outside to tighten my laces. I stand at the bus stop opposite and read the timetable. I hover at the crossing and review my recently deleted emails. I've never seen anyone go in or come out.

THIRTY-NINE, waiting for his face to change.

Forty: receptionist at the blood bank.

Forty-one: supervising nurse at the blood bank.

Forty-two.

Forty-three.

Baby's first birthday.

Seven hundred and twelve days after the abortion, I contact the charity for a second time to have my medical records released from the clinic.

I complete the paperwork quickly, in case I change my mind.

PLEASE DETAIL THE PURPOSE FOR WHICH YOUR MEDICAL RECORDS ARE REQUIRED.

Personal reasons, I write.

Seven hundred and fourteen days after the abortion, the medical records arrive by special courier. I tear into the packet:

PRIVATE AND CONFIDENTIAL

I stand over the blurred photocopies like I'm investigating a crime scene. I turn each page carefully, to preserve their order.

Data Subject   FOLLOW-UP CALL DECLINED   the opinion, formed in good faith   physical or mental health of the pregnant woman   INTRA-UTERINE PREGNANCY HAS BEEN CONFIRMED   100% SURE   AZITHROMYCIN MADE PATIENT FEEL SICK BUT DIDN'T VOMIT   MISOPROSTOL PV WITH CONSENT   AWARE TO GO STRAIGHT HOME DISCHARGE CRITERIA HAS BEEN MET   AFTERCARE PACK GIVEN   CLIENT AWARE OF HIGHER FAILURE RISK   COUNSELLING OFFERED   DECLINED   TRANS ABDOMINAL ULTRASOUND   TRANS VAGINAL ULTRASOUND   then the ultrasound images.

First thought: this is why they don't show you the screen.

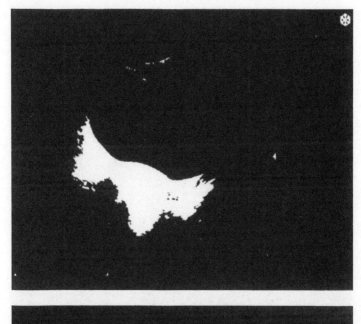

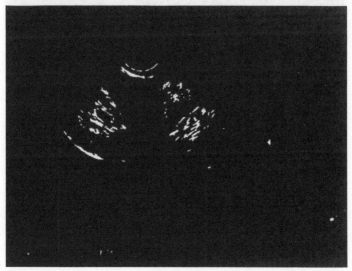

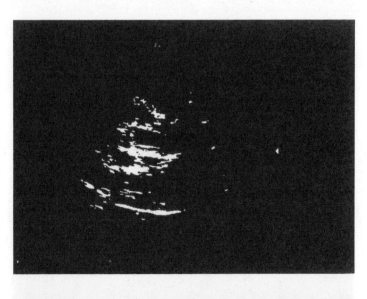

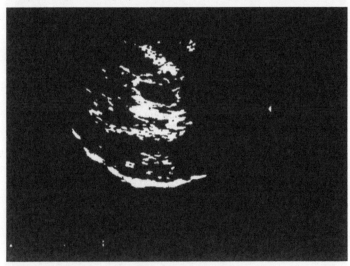

I lean over the photocopies. It feels like I might gag if I look too closely.

I turn back and forth, comparing the shapes.

nothing nothing someone kneeling hands together at their chest praying no waving a baby waving! with horns hello! that's it no nothing the number 9 a backwards, lowercase *g* a tiny rocket a turd there I see it

I put the ultrasounds back inside the envelope and go back to the start.

I already know I won't tell my family.

'You're my next of kin,' I mutter, handing FOUR the clipboard. He holds it against my back to fill out his details.

The nurse calls a number. FOUR nods at the empty seat. I race to sit down, like we're playing musical chairs. FOUR shuffles our bags across the floor between his feet and turns to face the television screen.

I consult the medical records over breakfast, when I get home from work, and before I go to bed.

It's difficult to remember what happened in what order. I was six weeks pregnant. The doctor had gone home. The pregnancy was paused for a day. I finished my work and had an abortion.

I go to the library after work and consult a medical textbook on pregnancy and childbirth.

GESTATION SAC PRESENT   YOLK SAC PRESENT

The dark, anechoic shape in the ultrasound is the gestational sac, which is formed in the first few weeks of pregnancy. The presence of a gestational sac is used to confirm a pregnancy before the embryo can be identified on an ultrasound. The yolk sac is formed inside the gestational sac and envelopes the embryo in amniotic fluid, providing sustenance until the placenta develops.

The nurse is writing on a form, which I decide not to look at. The consultation room is so small that our knees kiss. We press ourselves into the backs of our chairs.

'The doctor has gone home early, so unfortunately we can't start the procedure today.'

'But I was told there was an appointment available this afternoon.'

'The doctor has gone home, so you'll have to come back.'

'But I don't think I can wait. I'd really like to have the appointment today.'

'The doctor has gone home. You can't.'

'But I was *told*' (I grip my hands together) 'I could have the first part of the abortion today.'

'You'll have to come back tomorrow.'

I refuse to acknowledge that I'm crying.

'I don't think I can do that. Is there a different clinic I can go to?'

She says nothing.

'Why has the doctor gone home early? I booked an appointment.'

I'm stuck on this point. I don't believe the doctor isn't here somewhere.

'I booked this appointment.'

She watches me come to terms with it. The humiliation is complete.

'You'll have to come back for the first part tomorrow, but we can do some of the paperwork now, if you'd prefer.'

FIRST STAGE TREATMENTS

Drug	Dose	Route	Freq.	Drs sig	Batch no.	Expiry date	Given by	Time/Date
Mifegyne (Mifepristone)	200mg	O	Stat	▓▓▓	LF0696014	2019	▓▓▓	▓▓▓ 16:14
Metronidazole	1g	PR	Stat	▓▓▓	86	2020	self	▓▓▓ 16:15
Azithromycin	1g	O	TTO	▓▓▓	727116	2019	▓▓▓	To take at night

Azithromycin an antibiotic used to treat respiratory, skin, soft tissue, and other infections, including genital and eye infections caused by Chlamydia trachomatis. Possible side-effects include allergic reactions, nausea, and vomiting.

Metronidazole a drug used to treat infections of the urinary, genital, and digestive systems, acute ulcerative gingivitis, fungating wounds, and rosacea. Side-effects include digestive upsets and an unpleasant taste in the mouth.

Mifegyne (Mifepristone) a drug used to produce a medical abortion; it acts by blocking the action of progesterone, which is essential for maintaining pregnancy. It blocks the action of progesterone from the uterus, leading to the breakdown of the uterine lining and the softening, thinning, and widening of the cervix. Side-effects include faintness, headache, and vaginal bleeding.

O given or taken through or by way of the mouth.

PR by way of the rectum.

Statim immediately or without delay.

TTO to take out.

After the ultrasound, I ask if I can go to the toilet.

In the bathroom of the clinic, I look inside the medical waste bin as it slowly opens   wet paper towels, crushed medicine cup, inverted fingers of a latex glove   and closes.

SECOND STAGE TREATMENTS

Drug	Dose	Route	Freq.	Drs sig	Batch no.	Expiry date	Given by	Time/Date
Misoprostol	800mg	PV	Stat	▬	B14724	2019	▬	▬ 08:50
Diclofenac	100mg	PR	Stat	▬	142	2020	self	▬ 08:50
Codeine Phosphate	30mg	O	Stat	▬	1021936	2019	▬	▬ 08:50

Codeine Phosphate an opioid analgesic derived from morphine but less potent as a painkiller and sedative and less toxic. It is also used to suppress dry coughs and treat diarrhoea. Common side-effects include constipation, nausea, vomiting, dizziness, and drowsiness.

Diclofenac an anti-inflammatory drug used to relieve joint pain in osteoarthritis, rheumatoid arthritis, ankylosing spondylitis, acute gout, and actinic keratosis, and also for pain relief after surgery. Possible side-effects include abdominal pain, nausea, and diarrhoea; gastric ulceration can be prevented by administering diclofenac in combination with misoprostol.

Misoprostol a prostaglandin drug administered in the prevention and treatment of peptic ulcer, especially when caused by nonsteroidal anti-inflammatory drugs (NSAID), in which case it is given in conjunction with the NSAID. It is also used to terminate a pregnancy, being administered vaginally following mifepristone. Possible side-effects include diarrhoea.

PV by way of the vagina.

Taken orally, sublingually (under the tongue), or as a pessary (in the vagina), misoprostol is used to induce a miscarriage by stimulating uterine contractions.

It feels like I've just understood something. I sit and cry in the library.

Abortion in the United Kingdom is permitted under a legal exemption.

1. Medical termination of pregnancy.

(1) Subject to the provisions of this section, a person shall not be guilty of an offence under the law relating to abortion when a pregnancy is terminated by a registered medical practitioner if two registered medical practitioners are of the opinion, formed in good faith –

> (a) that the pregnancy has not exceeded its twenty-fourth week and that the continuance of the pregnancy would involve risk, greater than if the pregnancy were terminated, of injury to the physical or mental health of the pregnant woman or any existing children of her family; or

> (b) that the termination is necessary to prevent grave permanent injury to the physical or mental health of the pregnant woman; or

> (c) that the continuance of the pregnancy would involve risk to the life of the pregnant woman, greater than if the pregnancy were terminated; or

> (d) that there is a substantial risk that if the child were born it would suffer from such physical or mental abnormalities as to be seriously handicapped.

(2) In determining whether the continuance of a pregnancy would involve such risk of injury to health as is mentioned in paragraph (a) or (b) of subsection (1) of this section, account

may be taken of the pregnant woman's actual or reasonably foreseeable environment.

(3) Except as provided by subsection (4) of this section, any treatment for the termination of pregnancy must be carried out in a hospital vested in the Secretary of State for the purposes of his functions under the National Health Service Act 2006 or the National Health Service (Scotland) Act 1978 or in a hospital vested in a National Health Service trust or an NHS foundation trust or in a place approved for the purposes of this section by the Secretary of State.

(3A) The power under subsection (3) of this section to approve a place includes power, in relation to treatment consisting primarily in the use of such medicines as may be specified in the approval and carried out in such manner as may be so specified, to approve a class of places.

(4) Subsection (3) of this section, and so much of subsection (1) as relates to the opinion of two registered medical practitioners, shall not apply to the termination of a pregnancy by a registered medical practitioner in a case where he is of the opinion, formed in good faith, that the termination is immediately necessary to save the life or to prevent grave, permanent injury to the physical or mental health of the pregnant woman.

And why is it that you've decided today to have an abortion? Can you tell me why you've chosen to end the pregnancy? In your own words – when you're ready – can you explain why you want an abortion? *Why* do you feel you are unable to carry the pregnancy to term? Take a minute to compose yourself.

When my answer is incorrect, she rephrases the question. It's clear there is something I'm supposed to say, but I don't know what that is.

Because it's what I want to do   Because I feel very strongly that it's what I want to do   Because I'm pregnant and I don't want to be   Because I've chosen to have an abortion   Because I don't want to have a baby   Because I don't want to have a child   Because I am unable to support a child   Because I am unable to care for a child

I cowboy walk my chair backwards between answers. She checks my blood pressure while I mumble something about a career, then she takes my hand from my lap and pricks my index finger. She pours something on the blood and looks at it. She writes down the result.

The crying is slowing down the consultation. She stands up and shuffles past, her body sliding against the wall. The door closes behind her. I look around the room for a clue. The door opens and she drops a few tissues on the desk.

2. Notification.

(1) The Minister of Health in respect of England and Wales, and the Secretary of State in respect of Scotland, shall by statutory instrument make regulations to provide –

(a) for requiring any such opinion as is referred to in section 1 of this Act to be certified by the practitioners or practitioner concerned in such form and at such time as may be prescribed by the regulations, and for requiring the preservation and disposal of certificates made for the purposes of the regulations;

(b) for requiring any registered medical practitioner who terminates a pregnancy to give notice of the termination and such other information relating to the termination as may be so prescribed;

(c) for prohibiting the disclosure, except to such persons or for such purposes as may be so prescribed, of notices given or information furnished pursuant to the regulations.

(2) The information furnished in pursuance of regulations made by virtue of paragraph (b) of subsection (1) of this section shall be notified solely to the Chief Medical Officers of the Department of Health and Social Care, or of the Welsh Office, or of the Scottish Administration.

(3) Any person who wilfully contravenes or wilfully fails to comply with the requirements of regulations under subsection (1) of this section shall be liable on summary conviction to a fine not exceeding level 5 on the standard scale.

(4) Any statutory instrument made by virtue of this section shall be subject to annulment in pursuance of a resolution of either House of Parliament.

Before an abortion is carried out, a certificate must be completed by two registered medical practitioners. This form must be kept with the patient's records for three years from the date of termination.

ABORTION ACT 1967

Not to be destroyed within three years of the date of operation
Certificate to be completed before an abortion is
performed under Section 1(1) of the Act

CERTIFICATE A

I, ...

(Name and qualifications of practitioner in ...)

of ....

(Full address of practitioner)

Have/have not* seen/and examined* the pregnant woman to whom this certificate relates at

....

(full address of place at which patient was seen or examined)

on ....

and I ....

(Name and qualifications of practitioner in block capitals)

of ....

(Full address ...)

Have/have not* seen/and examined* the pregnant woman .... relates at

....

(Full address of place at which patient was seen or examined)

on ....

We hereby certify that we are of the opinion, formed in good faith, that in the case

of ....

of ....

(Usual place of residence of pregnant woman in block capitals)

(Ring appropriate letter(s))

A   the continuance of the pregnancy would involve risk to the life of the pregnant woman greater than if the pregnancy were terminated;

B   the termination is necessary to prevent grave permanent injury to the physical or mental health of the pregnant woman;

C   the pregnancy has NOT exceeded its 24th week and that the continuance of the pregnancy would involve risk, greater than if the pregnancy were terminated, of injury to the physical or mental health of the pregnant woman;

D   the pregnancy has NOT exceeded its 24th week and that the continuance of the pregnancy would involve risk, greater than if the pregnancy were terminated, of injury to the physical or mental health of any existing child(ren) of the family of the pregnant woman;

E   there is a substantial risk that if the child were born it would suffer from such physical or mental abnormalities as to be seriously handicapped.

This certificate of opinion is given before the commencement of the treatment for the termination of pregnancy to which it refers and relates to the circumstances of the pregnant woman's individual case.

Signed ....   Date ....

Signed ....   Date ....

* Delete as appropriate

Form HSA1 (revised 1991)

The nurse is shielding the checklist. We have reached an impasse. I want her to tell me what to say. I try to speak slowly and clearly.

I believe, very strongly, that there would be serious, lasting repercussions to my mental health, in the short and long term, if I were to carry the pregnancy to term   I feel that I would be at a great risk to myself, if I had to continue the pregnancy I think I would experience extreme mental distress, and would hurt myself, if I were unable to have an abortion

I have finally admitted it. Disbelief becomes anger. I wipe my face and sit up straight.

I look up the two doctors who approved the procedure on the internet. I realise I'd forgotten to include them in the list.

Forty-four, forty-five.

'You're six weeks pregnant.'

'But I can't be.'

'Well, you are. Six weeks pregnant.'

I start to cry. She moves on to the next piece of paperwork.

'I'm not saying I'm not pregnant, but I didn't have sex six weeks ago –'

'Look –'

'I had sex three and a half weeks ago.'

'You're six weeks pregnant.'

MATURITY < 6 WEEKS ≈ 5 WEEKS

My time-travelling pregnancy. I can see the shape of the nurse's arm in her handwriting.

I learn that the forty-week gestational period is counted from the first day of the last period, not the date of conception.

I was six to five weeks pregnant, but it didn't exist for two of those weeks.

FORTY-SEVEN, who brings three strangers – FORTY-EIGHT, FORTY-NINE and FIFTY – out for drinks, and in the middle of the conversation I realise he's told them.

'FORTY-SEVEN says you're writing a book about abortion?'

Fifty-one.

FIFTY-TWO, who I tell is fifty-two.

I spread the pages out on the table.

ibuprofen suppository   'When you're ready, I need you to take the tablet out of the blister pack yourself'   'Sign here' 'Do you understand that this drug is being administered out of licence?'   'Yes'   'Sign to say that you're aware of the risks'   'Come back tomorrow'   I think I want to hurt myself azithromycin before bed   ibuprofen walking to the clinic codeine in a medicine cup   'OK we're ready to start now' 'Do you understand that this drug is being administered out of licence?'   'No'   'It means it's being prescribed outside the terms of what it's licensed for in the UK'   'OK'   'Sign here' 'pessaries'   'like a dissolving film'   'soften and open'   'We use two, just to be sure'   'Take off your trousers and lie on the bed' 'I'm going to put them on the tip of my finger and place them inside your vagina'   'right next to the cervix'   'OK and just stay still like that for a minute'

17 July 2019

DISCHARGE CHECK LIST

All medications administered as prescribed	*YES*
Client aware to perform pregnancy test	*YES*
Client aware to contact clinic (if positive)	*YES*
Aftercare leaflet and advice given	*YES*
Has contraception been prescribed?	*NO*
State contraceptive issued	*NONE*

If not, reason why no contraception has been issued:

DECLINES ALL CONTRACEPTION

Let me put it this way: When you leave the clinic today, you must be on some form of contraception. We need to make sure that you are using contraception when you leave the clinic.

She takes out a colourful chart to demonstrate that I will be fertile 'immediately' after the abortion. I cross-reference the chart with the rule about not having sex.

I explain that I've tried lots of different kinds of contraception and I don't want to choose something at random, right now. I explain that I'm not in a relationship. She smirks. I explain that I'd like to make an informed decision, at some point in the future, when I'm not so upset. I tell her I'll arrange to see a doctor next month. I tell her I'll arrange to see a doctor in two weeks.

Preferred future contraception?

DECLINES TO COMMENT

Have you had unprotected sex in the last twenty-four hours? Did the condom break? Why did you decide not to use a condom? What were the circumstances surrounding your decision? Have you consumed any alcohol in the last twenty-four hours? If the alcohol you have consumed makes you vomit, you must return to the pharmacy to purchase a repeat prescription Have you used emergency contraception before? Emergency contraception is not contraception When was the last time you used it? How many times have you used it? The pharmacist has gone home for the day We're closing for lunch Can you come back later? The total cost today is £25 ('I'm not sure, I'm sorry') That's £28.25 when you're ready, please ('I got carried away, I'm sorry') That'll be £30 today ('it's been a while, I thought you might be on the pill or something') Is your boyfriend here with you? How many times have you taken this before? Have you consumed any alcohol today? How much alcohol did you consume yesterday? Have you ever been pregnant before? Do you understand the risks of ectopic pregnancy? If you vomit, which is possible given your recent consumption of alcohol, you must come back and take it again In that instance, you would need to pay the full cost again Unfortunately, there's no evidence to back up your claim that the pill made you put on weight Have you ever been depressed before? Have you tried a different pill? Do you often have periods of low mood, of feeling 'blue'? Have you tried this combination? Have you tried this combination? Have you tried lavender oil?

Have you tried just getting a good night's sleep? What kind of migraines? Are you sure they're real migraines and not headaches? What makes you think that they're migraines? When were they diagnosed as migraines? Have you tried taking a week off the pill? Have you tried never taking a week off? Have you considered getting the injection? When do you want to have children? How old are you? The swelling in your arm is a completely natural response to the implant don't touch it The purple mark in your arm is a bruise from the insertion process, which went exactly as planned don't touch it The purple mark in your arm is an infection, which should clear up in a few days The purple mark in your arm is a vein that has been pushed to the surface by the implant The purple mark in your arm is nothing to worry about, because only your boyfriend sees that part of your body I want to remind you that there may be some pain, spotting, cramping, and bleeding after the IUS has been inserted It may make your periods shorter or longer It may make your periods more or less painful We can prescribe drugs for the bleeding We can prescribe drugs for the pain We can prescribe drugs to deal with the side-effects of the drugs you are taking because of the bleeding and pain Have you tried having a nice long bath? Is it proper bleeding? How many teaspoons, would you say?

More drinking. I stand outside and check my phone. I scroll through my contacts. It's been two years since the abortion. It's three months since the abortion. It's four hours since the abortion. No new messages.

When I get back to the table, I ask FIFTEEN if he knows the difference between an embryo, a foetus, and a baby. FOURTEEN laughs nervously, anticipating a punchline.

I stop at the shops on the way home and buy chocolate and biscuits and sweets. I eat everything.

I check the handwriting and signatures one last time.

I understand that there are other options available: surgical procedures under general or local anaesthetic

I understand that an early medical abortion is a two-stage process

I understand that once I commence treatment, if I change my mind and decide to continue with the pregnancy there is a high risk of complications

I am also aware that there is a high risk of incomplete miscarriage or infection if I do not attend for the second stage of treatment

In the event that I do not attend the second stage appointment the clinic will contact my GP and inform them that the treatment is incomplete

I am aware that the first stage treatment may cause nausea, dizziness, headaches, abdominal cramps, diarrhoea, bleeding

Following administration of the medication for both parts of my treatment, I will go home immediately

I understand that the miscarriage may start to happen as quickly as thirty minutes after the second stage appointment

I understand that I must not go home on any form of public transport, drive myself, or walk home after the second stage appointment

I understand that there is a high risk that I may see products of conception

I destroy my copy of the medical records.

I rinse the clot off the applicator.

[----] presses my body against the glass. I can taste my strawberry conditioner in his beard. I lean back under the water and he smooths his hands over my hair.

I run at the reservoir. The layer of flies and dust and algae on the surface disappears. The dirty water rushes up my swimming costume.

17 March 2020

The clinic destroys the medical records.